JOURNEYS

Migrating with Arctic Tern

Thessaly Catt

PowerKiDS press

New York

Published in 2011 by The Rosen Publishing Group, Inc.
29 East 21st Street, New York, NY 10010

First Edition

Editor: Amelie von Zumbusch
Book Design: Ashley Burrell

Photo Credits: Cover, pp. 4, 14, 16 Shutterstock.com; p. 5 Anthony Bannister/Getty Images; p. 6 Richard Packwood/Getty Images; p. 7 © www.iStockphoto.com/Dmitry Deshevykh; p. 8 Paul Nicklen/Getty Images; p. 9 © www.iStockphoto.com/oversnap; p. 11 Arctic-Images/Getty Images; pp. 12–13, 22 Norbert Rosing/Getty Images; p. 15 Graham Wren/Getty Images; p. 17 (top) © www.iStockphoto.com/David Thyberg; pp. 17 (bottom), 18 iStockphoto/Thinkstock; p. 19 Pal Hermansen/Getty Images; pp. 20–21 © waldhaeusl.com/age fotostock.

Library of Congress Cataloging-in-Publication Data

Catt, Thessaly.
 Migrating with the Arctic Tern / by Thessaly Catt. — 1st ed.
     p. cm. — (Animal journeys)
 Includes index.
 ISBN 978-1-4488-2542-4 (library binding) — ISBN 978-1-4488-2668-1 (pbk.) —
 ISBN 978-1-4488-2669-8 (6-pack)
 1. Arctic tern—Juvenile literature. 2. Arctic tern—Migration—Juvenile literature. I. Title.
 QL696.C46C38 2011
 598.3'38—dc22
                              2010025389

Manufactured in the United States of America

CPSIA Compliance Information: Batch #WW11PK: For Further Information contact Rosen Publishing, New York, New York at 1-800-237-9932

Contents

Many animals make long journeys every year. They travel huge distances to find food or warm weather or to stay safe from **predators**. They fly, walk, or swim hundreds or thousands of miles (km). However these animals travel, though,

Not all arctic terns take the same route when they migrate. For this reason, the lengths they travel can be different. Some travel as far as 49,700 miles (79,984 km) in a year!

These arctic terns are migrating. They are flying along the coast of Namibia, in southern Africa.

their journeys are called migrations. The animal that makes Earth's longest migration is the arctic tern.

Arctic terns are a kind of seabird. They travel around 44,000 miles (70,900 km) in a year. In an arctic tern's lifetime, it will fly about 1.5 million miles (2.4 million km). This means that each arctic tern flies about the distance of three trips to the Moon!

There are several kinds of terns. The easiest way to tell that a tern is an arctic tern is to see if it has a bright red beak.

Arctic terns are medium-sized birds. They are related to seagulls. Adult arctic terns are about 12 to 15 inches (30–38 cm) long. The birds measure between 30 and 33 inches (76–84 cm) from wing tip to wing tip. Arctic terns weigh about 3.5 ounces (100 g).

Adult male and female arctic terns look nearly the same. Both have red beaks, legs, and feet. Their beaks, also called bills, are very sharp. The terns' feet are webbed. They have forked tails. In summer, arctic terns have mostly gray bodies, with black heads and white cheeks. Between December and March, their heads are lighter in color and their beaks are darker.

Their body shape and long wings and tails make arctic terns quick fliers. They also make it easy for terns to change direction quickly while flying.

Two Summers Each Year

Arctic terns **breed** in the Northern **Hemisphere**, in places such as Alaska, Canada, Greenland, Iceland, Denmark, and northern Russia. In order to escape winter in the Northern Hemisphere, they migrate south to Antarctica each fall. This

These arctic terns are resting on an ice floe in northern Canada. Ice floes are big pieces of ice floating in the ocean.

In Antarctica, arctic terns spend most of their time along the edges of large sheets of ice called pack ice. Other seabirds, such as penguins, live there, too.

is because it is summer in the Southern Hemisphere when it is winter in the Northern Hemisphere.

Each April, arctic terns start their journeys back north to their breeding grounds. There, they spend another summer. Arctic terns spend most of their lives flying because these journeys between the Arctic and Antarctica take such a long time.

The Arctic Tern's Fall Migration

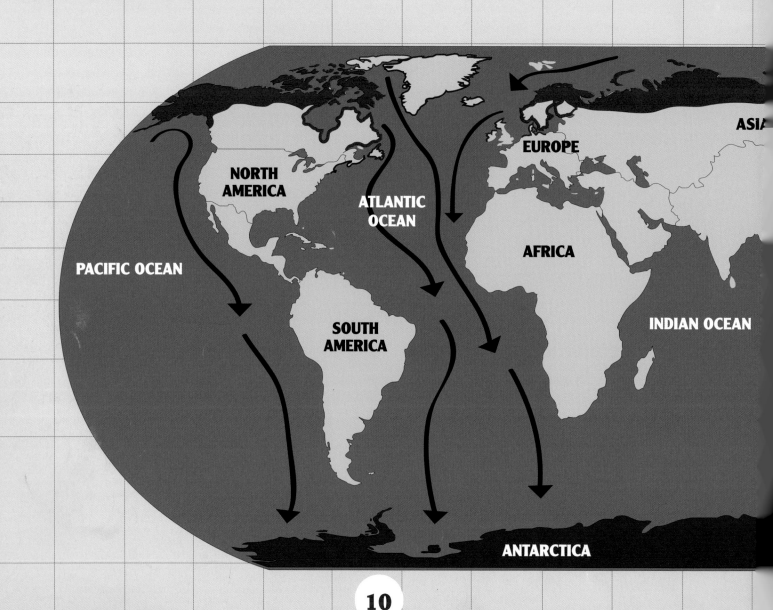

NORTH AMERICA

EUROPE

ASIA

ATLANTIC OCEAN

AFRICA

PACIFIC OCEAN

SOUTH AMERICA

INDIAN OCEAN

ANTARCTICA

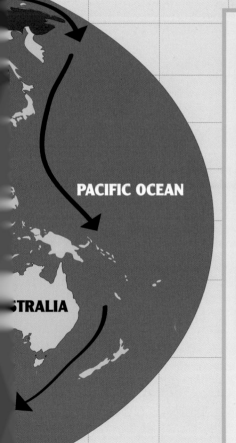
Map: Arctic terns take many routes to reach their wintering grounds. Though it is summer when the terns are there, these Antarctic grounds are called wintering grounds. This is because the terns go there to escape the Arctic winter.

PACIFIC OCEAN

STRALIA

These arctic terns are spending the summer in Iceland. Many arctic terns nest in Iceland.

Arctic terns generally reach their breeding grounds in May or early June. The terns breed along the coast, on islands, and on the Arctic **tundra**. A male arctic tern tries to win a female **mate** by catching a fish and bringing it to her. This is called a fish flight. Scientists think that arctic terns stay with their mates for life.

After mating, arctic terns quickly build nests on land near either salt water or freshwater. The nests are shallow holes in the sand or dirt. The female arctic terns lay their eggs there. Arctic terns build their nests close together in big groups, called colonies.

This male arctic tern is bringing his mate a fish. His fish flight is part of his courtship, or system for winning a mate.

This is an arctic tern egg. The egg's colors and speckles make it harder to see against the ground.

Female terns lay between one and three eggs at a time. The eggs are greenish brown and **speckled**. Both parents keep the nest safe from predators and sit on the eggs to keep them warm.

The eggs **hatch** about 22 to 25 days after they are laid. The parents take turns caring for the babies, called hatchlings. The adult terns bring the hatchlings food, such as small fish. Hatchlings start to fly about 22 days after they hatch. This is called fledging. After they learn to fly, young terns stay with their parents for a month or two more. Then, they are ready to care for themselves. Arctic terns can live for up to 30 years.

Here, an adult tern is looking after its chick. Arctic tern chicks can be either gray or brown.

Arctic terns are **carnivores**. This means that they are meat eaters. They hunt for insects, shrimp, **crustaceans**, and small fish, such as polar cod. Most of the terns' hunting is done in shallow waters along coasts.

This arctic tern has caught a small fish. Arctic terns eat many kinds of small fish, such as sand eels and capelin.

Although arctic terns are very good at hunting for fish, they are not good swimmers. This is because their webbed feet are very small. In order to catch fish, the terns **hover** above the water, looking for small

When they fish, arctic terns catch fish with their sharp, strong beaks.

Arctic terns feed their hatchlings for about a month. Then the hatchlings must find their own food.

fish to catch. Then, they quickly dive into the water after the fish. Once they have caught the fish, the terns fly away with it.

Attacking Predators

Arctic foxes, such as this one, sometimes eat arctic tern eggs and hatchlings.

Migrating arctic terns do not often have to worry about predators. However, when they are nesting in their Arctic breeding grounds, adult arctic terns must worry about keeping their eggs and hatchlings safe. Cats, foxes, skunks, and other birds, such as gulls and skuas, all eat arctic tern eggs and hatchlings.

Arctic terns quickly attack any predators that enter their breeding grounds. Once they spot a predator, a group of arctic terns will dive at the predator's head over and over. This is called mobbing. They also cry loudly, hoping to scare the predator away. They are very **aggressive** attackers.

This arctic tern is loudly defending its nest. Arctic terns will attack predators many times their size.

Tracking Arctic Terns

Scientists track the migration of arctic terns with **geolocators**. They put these tiny objects on the terns' legs. The geolocators tell scientists where a tern is two times each day. Though scientists have used geolocators to track migrating animals for years, they have only recently made ones that are light enough to use on arctic terns.

Before they started using geolocators, scientists thought that arctic terns traveled only about 24,000 miles (39,000 km) a year. Now, scientists have learned that arctic terns fly in zigzag patterns between Antarctica and the Arctic Ocean instead of in straight lines. This means that the distance they travel is much greater!

Scientists put geolocators on rings like the one this arctic tern is wearing on its leg.

Arctic Terns in a Changing World

Arctic terns may face some problems in the future. **Climate change** may throw off the birds' migratory **routes**. Spills from oil wells in the ocean could also cause problems for arctic terns. Oil spills can pollute the waters and shores where terns fish and nest.

One of the things scientists hope to learn about arctic terns is how they find their way when they are migrating.

However, arctic tern **populations** are not yet in danger of dying out. About one million arctic terns continue to mate and migrate around the world every year. Scientists look forward to learning new things about these incredible birds now that they can track the terns' migratory routes.

Glossary

aggressive (uh-GREH-siv) Ready to fight.

breed (BREED) To make babies.

carnivores (KAHR-neh-vorz) Animals that eat other animals.

climate change (KLY-mut CHAYNJ) Changes in Earth's weather that were caused by things people did.

crustaceans (krus-TAY-shunz) Animals that have no backbone, have hard shells and other body parts, and live mostly in water.

geolocators (jee-oh-LOH-kay-turz) Small objects that are put on animals to track their movements.

hatch (HACH) To come out of an egg.

hemisphere (HEH-muh-sfeer) Half of Earth.

hover (HUH-ver) To fly in place in the air.

mate (MAYT) A partner for making babies.

populations (pop-yoo-LAY-shunz) Groups of animals or people living in the same place.

predators (PREH-duh-terz) Animals that kill other animals for food.

routes (ROOTS) The paths people or animals take to get somewhere.

speckled (SPEH-keld) Having speckles, or spots.

tundra (TUN-druh) The icy land of the coldest parts of the world.

Index

A
Alaska, 8

B
beaks, 7

C
carnivores, 16
climate change, 22
crustaceans, 16

D
distance(s), 4–5, 21

E
eggs, 13–15, 18

F
fish, 12, 15–17, 22
food, 4, 15

G
geolocators, 20–21

L
lifetime, 5

N
Northern Hemisphere,
8–9

P
populations, 22

predator(s), 4, 14,
18–19

R
routes, 22

S
seabird, 5
seagulls, 6

T
tails, 7
tundra, 12

W
weather, 4

Web Sites

Due to the changing nature of Internet links, PowerKids Press has developed an online list of Web sites related to the subject of this book. This site is updated regularly. Please use this link to access the list:
www.powerkidslinks.com/anjo/arctern/